Thermostat

of

HOPE

by

Charles Capps

*Unless otherwise indicated, all Scripture
quotations are taken from the New King James
Version NKJV of the Bible.*

*Scripture quotations marked (NASB) are from
the New American Standard Bible. Copyright ©
the Lockman Foundation 1960, 1962, 1963, 1968,
1971, 1972, 1973, 1975, 1977. Used by permission.*

16   15   14   5   4   3   2   1

The Thermostat of HOPE
ISBN 13: 978-1-937578-30-5
Previously entitled HOPE: A Partner to Faith
ISBN 13: 978-0-9819574-4-9
Formerly ISBN 13: 978-0-89274-396-4
Formerly ISBN 10: 0-89274-396-4

Copyright © 1986 by Charles Capps
PO Box 69, England, Arkansas 72046

Published by Capps Publishing
PO Box 69, England, Arkansas 72046

HOPE

A Partner To Faith

Now faith is the substance of things hoped for, the evidence of things not seen.

Hebrews 11:1

Faith is the substance of things, but hope is a necessity. Sometimes people say, "You don't get anything by hoping." And that's true to a certain extent, for there is no substance to hope.

But hope is a very important partner to faith. Hope is the goal-setter. **Faith is *the substance of things hoped for.*** The substance of "things" -what things? The things you **hoped for**. What do we hope for? We hope for the things that God has given us.

That's why the Bible says in Hebrews 11:6, **But without faith it is impossible to please him...** God is not pleased when we don't enter into the provisions that He made for us. Some things we will never enter into except through faith. God's willingness is multiplied to us through the knowledge of God. We must know what God has given, or we can't have faith in that promise.

> **Grace and peace be multiplied to you in the knowledge of God and of Jesus our Lord,**

> **As His divine power has given to us all things that *pertain* to life and godliness, through the knowledge of Him who called us by glory and virtue**

2 Peter 1:2-3

Hope Is Necessary

Hope is a partner to faith. You are reading this book because you hope to receive some insight into hope and faith. But hope alone will not give you that insight. Yet, if it wasn't for hope, you wouldn't have opened this book.

When people who are sick come to a healing service, they hope to be healed. If they didn't have hope, **they wouldn't come**

for prayer. Since faith is the substance of **things hoped for,** then **there must be some hope**, or there wouldn't be anything for faith **to give substance to.**

This will explain to you why some have died, even though they were saying all the right things. Others say, "I just don't understand why they died." It could be that they gave up hope.

God's Word Gave Hope to Abraham

Look at what Abraham did when there was no hope.

(As it is written, "I have made you a father of many nations") in the presence of Him whom he believed—God, who gives life to the dead and calls those things which do not exist as though they did;

Who, contrary to hope, in hope believed, so that he became the father of many nations, according to what was spoken, "So shall your descendants be."

Romans 4:17-18

When there was no hope, Abraham believed in hope. There are people today who have no hope **medically.** Doctors have done all they can do. When the doctor says there is no hope, do what Abraham did: **go to the Word of God and get supernatural hope.** He decided to agree with God. That's what we are doing when we make a decision to begin to speak and confess the Scriptures out loud. We are coming over to God's point of view by saying what God declared about us.

Some might say, **"There is no hope, so you might as well give up."** You can **always** go to the Word of God and get some hope. I don't care if it's physical, financial, or spiritual. When your situation **seems** to be hopeless, go to the Word of God. God's Word is hope for you.

Hope is a goal-setter. You must have a goal. If you don't set any goals, or if you don't know where you are going, then **how will you know when you get there?** How long will it take you to get there? You don't know where you are going, and you don't know how to get there, but a goal gives direction.

Faith is the substance of things **hoped for. There must be some direction for faith to flow; something for faith to fulfill. Hope sets the direction. Faith is the energy substance that flows to it.** Some have said, "Well, I'm just waiting on God. I'm believing God."

Some of those people have been waiting for years, and they haven't done anything. They are not waiting on God – God has been waiting on them. They have made a decision by doing nothing.

When there was no hope, Abraham decided to believe in hope. **He made a decision** to believe God's Word. That is where his hope came from - the Word of God. Don't try to use faith where hope should be, and don't try to use hope where faith should be. **Hope has no substance.** Faith is the substance of the thing hoped for.

So there must be **faith and hope.** They are partners. They go together. **Faith is the divine energy of God.** It comes by hearing God's Word. It is the **substance of things** desired.

We must learn to sow the seed of

God's Word. Words are seeds. We speak the Word of God - the promise of God - into our hearts, and it springs forth and grows up: **...first the blade, then the head, after that the full grain in the head.** In Mark 4:28, it was established by Jesus that the heart was the production center. Jesus called it the soil.

Revelation Comes by the Spirit

We talk about the heart being the production center, and Paul adds some light to this subject in his first letter to the Corinthian church.

> **But as it is written: "Eye has not seen, nor ear heard, nor have entered into the heart of man the things which God has prepared for those who love Him."**

> **But God has revealed them to us through His Spirit. For the Spirit searches all things, yes, the deep things of God.**

> 1 Corinthians 2:9-10

Eye has not seen, ear has not heard. How many times have you heard people quote this scripture and say, "You never know what God is going to do." But **you will know,** if you read verse 10, *But God has revealed them to us through His Spirit.*

He is telling us that these things won't enter into the heart of man through the natural five senses realm. You cannot get revelation knowledge into your spirit through the five physical senses. But **God reveals things** to us by His Spirit.

God's Spirit bears witness with our spirit and reveals things by revelation knowledge that we can't get any other way. God will do everything He said He would do. God will do everything He promised. **He will do everything you believe Him to do, if your faith is based on His Word.** But these things have not entered into the heart of man through the **natural eye** or the **natural ear.** They entered into the heart of man by revelation. God has revealed them to us **by His Spirit.** God **did** reveal them, but not through the five physical senses.

God has an avenue through which He reveals things and sometimes it bypasses the carnal mind. God reveals things to our spirit by the Holy Spirit. He is our teacher and guide.

The Human Spirit Searches

In 1 Corinthians 2:10, both uses of the word "Spirit" are capitalized. The first part of the verse says, **But God has revealed them to us through *His Spirit.*** This is referring to the Holy Spirit. But where it says, **for the Spirit searches all things, yes, the deep things of God;** that is not referring to the Holy Spirit. That refers to the human spirit - your spirit. Proverbs says it this way:

> **The spirit of a man is the lamp of the Lord, searching all the inner depths of his heart.**

Proverbs 20:27

The human spirit is the light bulb that God uses to enlighten you. God's Spirit bears witness with your spirit. God's

Spirit bears witness with our spirits and enlightens our spirits.*

For *the Spirit* searches all things, yes, the deep things of God. I believe the Apostle Paul is referring here to the human spirit, for the Holy Spirit does not need to search the things of God. The Holy Spirit already knows the things of God. **It's the human spirit that searches the things of God.**

When you are asleep, the seeds you have planted in the heart are producing. And you don't really know how. All you did was sow them, and go to bed and get up.

Your Spirit Knows -
God's Spirit Knows

For what man knows the things of a man except the spirit of the man which is in him? Even so no one knows the things of God except the Spirit of God.

1 Corinthians 2:11

---

* The book *The Light of Life in the Spirit of Man* by Charles Capps has additional teaching on this topic.

God's Spirit knows all about God, and your spirit knows all about you. If you get your spirit in contact with God's Spirit, **you have tapped the source of all knowledge.**

> **Now we have received, not the spirit of the world, but the Spirit who is from God, that we might know the things that have been freely given to us by God.**
>
> 1 Corinthians 2:12

We need to connect this with what Paul said in verse nine. **Eye has not seen, nor ear heard, nor have entered into the heart of man...** that is, through the natural five senses.

You didn't see it by the physical eye, you didn't hear it with the natural ear, but God revealed it. It came by revelation of the Holy Spirit into your spirit. **The spirit searches all things, yes, the deep things of God.** So, after you **sow the seed into your heart,** while you sleep at night, **your spirit searches for the wisdom and revelation of God** in regard to ways and means to bring that seed to production.

Then you will wake up some morning with an idea that came from the Spirit of God into your heart, and you won't know when or how it came.

Verse 12 states that **God gave us the human spirit** so that He could reveal the things of God to us.

> **These things we also speak, not in words which man's wisdom teaches but which the Holy Spirit teaches, comparing spiritual things with spiritual.**

> **But the natural man does not receive the things of the Spirit of God, for they are foolishness to him; nor can he know them, because they are spiritually discerned.**

> 1 Corinthians 2:13-14

Comparing Spiritual Things

We must compare spiritual things with spiritual. The spirit of man contacts the Spirit of God to find revelation knowledge of these things concerning our everyday lives. We don't gain revelation knowledge through the carnal mind. It comes into the human spirit.

The natural physical body does not receive the things of the Spirit of God; but the things of the Spirit of God are received into the human spirit, which is the production center.

> **But he who is spiritual judges all things, yet he himself is rightly judged by no one.**
>
> 1 Corinthians 2:15

Who is **he that is spiritual?** Now, remember, he said to compare spiritual things with spiritual. He that is spiritual judges all things. The part of you that is spiritual is the inner man or the spirit. Your spirit judges all things.

Your human spirit may pick up things about other people that you do not understand with your natural mind. It has not been revealed to you through the eye or the natural ear or any of the five senses. At times, you sense some things and you don't know how you know, but you know that you know that you know.

Enlightened by Your Spirit

You may meet someone and it seems as though your spirit says, "Get away from them. Don't have anything to do with them," and you don't know why. Your spirit will draw up in a knot. Your spirit was "searching all things" and it found something and was warning you.

He that is spiritual judges all things, but he himself is judged of no man. Your spirit **senses** something about the person's spirit, but you yourself cannot **judge** what is in their spirit. You can only judge their actions.

> For "who has known the mind of the Lord that he may instruct Him?" But we have the mind of Christ.

1 Corinthians 2:16

We gain the knowledge of the mind of Christ by the Holy Spirit, through the human spirit.

The spirit of man truly is the light of the Lord. Let's put these two thoughts together. In Mark 4:26, the heart of man is referred to as the soil. It is where you plant the seed of the Word of God so it can produce.

It is the Spirit that reveals things to you and gains the knowledge. **God has given us His Spirit so that we might receive the things of the Spirit of God.** The heart is the reception center.

When you speak words, you are sowing seed. When you are speaking the Word of God, **you are sowing incorruptible seed.** That seed will not fail. Yet it is possible for your action or inaction to cause a harvest failure. The seed will not fail. But what we do with the seed could cause a production failure.

A Lazy Man Prophesies
His Own Doom

In Proverbs 22:13, we find this statement; **The lazy man says, "There is a lion outside! I shall be slain in the streets!"**

The lazy man is one who isn't going to do anything. He just sits there and says, ''I'll

16

be eaten." He doesn't even run. He could at least make an effort to get out of the street. **But he prophesies his own doom.**

Those who don't act on the Word of God are doing that all the time. They say, "Well, you know, we're all going under." "Nothing ever works out for me." "The world's going to blow up in one big atomic blast, and we're all going to be doomed." The lazy man prophesies his own doom.

Natural Things Reflect Spiritual Things

We are capable of conceiving God's Word in our spirit, bringing forth production of what God said in His Word. Remember, hope is a goal-setter.

Sometimes, when we see these things in the Bible, we tend to take them completely out of their natural setting. When Jesus talked about sowing a seed, He didn't take it away from the soil and say, "This is a spiritual thing."

We make a serious mistake when we totally separate the natural from the spiritual. God's Word is spiritual, but it works like a natural seed. The heart of man is spiritual, but it works like natural soil.

Let me give you an illustration of how the heart is designed to produce. Let's bring it down to the natural level where we can all understand it. There probably is a piece of equipment at your house called a heating and air conditioning unit. It is the heart of the heating and cooling system.

That unit has been designed by an engineer to control the temperature of your house. That's all it was designed to do. It is designed to produce whatever you dial into that little thermostat on the wall, which we will call a goal-setter. The heart of that unit was designed to produce whatever temperature you dial into that thermostat.

The numbers on that thermostat represent degrees of temperature. Let's say it is 100 degrees outside, and you want the temperature to be 70 degrees inside. Your job would be to turn that goal-setter to 70 degrees. As long as it is kept on 70 degrees, **that unit will work night and day to see that the goal is reached.**

You wouldn't have to fast and pray that it would get cool in your house. The unit knows how to do it. That is what it was designed to do. You would simply dial the goal-setter, and it would send an impulse to the heart of that unit and say, "Get us some cold air in here. It's hot." With the thermostat on 70 degrees when it's 100 degrees outside, you have created a problem for the heart of that unit. But it can handle it. That is all it knows to do, but it can do it well.

That unit won't wash your clothes, it won't cook your dinner, it won't clean your house. It wasn't designed to do those things. It was designed for one purpose: to produce what you have dialed into the goal-setter.

The Heart Produces

Now let's relate this to the heart of man. The heart of the heating-cooling unit is like the heart of man. **You must set the goal for the thing you want produced.** Faith is the substance of things hoped for, and hope is the goal-setter.

Hope works in the head. What you continue to speak becomes your goal. Your head is the goal-setter. When there is no hope, there is no goal set for the better – although "no hope" sets negative goals.

Like the thermostat on the wall, your spoken words send an impulse into your spirit.

By saying, **"In the name of Jesus, by His stripes I am healed. I am redeemed from the curse of the Law, and I forbid sickness and disease in this body,"** you set your goal on healing.

What are you doing by that action? Someone may say, "You are lying, because you are sick." You may be sick all right, but the purpose of speaking God's Word is to set your goal and plant seed. Some people don't understand how you can say you're healed by the stripes of Jesus when you are hurting. But you must decide to establish that goal regardless of present circumstances.

Let's relate this concept to the way a thermostat works. Let's say it is 90 degrees in your house, and you come in and turn the thermostat to 70 degrees. Someone might say, "Hey! You can't do that. That's a lie. It's not 70 degrees in here."

But it's not a lie. That's the way to make the heating-cooling unit work the way it was designed. That's the reason you set it on 70. You are calling for that temperature. You are calling for the temperature that is not manifest. That is the way the system is designed, and that is the only way it will work. If you set 90 degrees in the thermostat when it is 90 degrees already, there will be no change. The unit will remain inactive, producing nothing.

The Heart Is True to
Demands Placed On It

Surely no one would be foolish enough in natural things to argue with you when you turned the thermostat to 70 degrees. But they will when you set your goal on God's promises.

Some will argue that you are lying. You have to give some time and meditation to these things to fully understand the design of the heart (spirit) of man.

It's easy to understand the way that goal setter (thermostat) works. By looking at this example, it's easier to understand that faith and confession work that way on your heart. You may not believe it works that way. You may not like it, **but that's the way it works.**

No one would argue with you about turning that thermostat to achieve the desired temperature, and no one would call you a liar. They understand that it will be 70 degrees in the room in a few minutes.

The heart (spirit) of man is like the heart of that heating-cooling unit. It is designed by God to produce the very thing that you plant in it. You plant it or set the goal by speaking it.

When you first hear a recording of your voice, you usually think it is someone else. You can't believe it is you, because you have been hearing your voice mostly with your inner ear. Your voice is picked up by the inner ear and fed directly into your spirit.

When you heard the recording of your voice, you heard it for the first time totally with the outer ear and could not believe it was you.

God designed you that way, so your voice would feed the impulse of what you desired right down into the garden spot, the heart, which is the soil. (Luke 13:18-19.) There it will produce what you are speaking. It is also renewing your mind as you are confessing God's Word.

Suppose someone turns the thermostat to 70 degrees and then, in a little while, they turn it to 95. Then they turn it to 60. It will not work properly that way. It will probably blow a fuse. It is not designed to be flipped from one extreme to the other all at once. It will blow a circuit.

Someone might say, "Who would be dumb enough to do that?" Christians do that all of the time. They start making faith confessions: "Glory to God, my needs are met according to His riches in glory by Christ Jesus." They say that for a few days, then they look at circumstances and say, "Dear God, it's never going to happen. We will never get these debts paid. I don't know what we are going to do."

Well, they just changed the thermostat. You have to set it where you want it and leave it there. That unit will work day and night to produce what you have dialed into it. It will never argue with you.

The Unit Does Not
Make Decisions

Have you ever heard a heating-cooling unit say, "No, I'm not sending cold air; you need hot air, so I'm lighting up the fire to send you some heat?"

If it did that, we would have to say, "Well, you never know what that unit is going to do. It has a mind of its own."

But it doesn't work that way. It is consistent. It always produces the very thing you call for, and that is how the heart (spirit) of man is designed.

> **The spirit of a man *is* the lamp of the Lord, searching all the inner depths of his heart.**
>
> Proverbs 20:27

> **You will also declare a thing, and it will be established for you; so light will shine on your ways.**
>
> Job 22:28

Mark 4:26 tells you the way it works. It is as if a man cast the seed into the ground. That is setting the goal. A seed to a farmer is a goalsetter. If you want to know what goal you have set for your garden, just look and see what seed you have planted. You plant the seed, and it works. You go to bed and get up. You don't have to hope to God that it will work. It will work because it is designed that way. The substance is in the seed itself.

Thermostats Have No Substance

Suppose someone who had never seen a thermostat or a heating-cooling unit saw you turn the thermostat to 70 degrees when the room was 90 degrees. When it began to get cool, he would wonder why it was getting so cool. He would want to know what you did.

"What is that little box on the wall?"

You say, "That is a thermostat."

"A thermostat. Where can I get one?"

You see what he has in mind. He goes down to the hardware store and buys a thermostat. He goes out to his cabin and nails it on the wall. Then he turns it to 70 degrees and sits down and waits.

He will have a long wait, because the goalsetter does not have the ability to cool his cabin. It is only a goal-setter. There is no substance in the thermostat to cool a room. Yet it establishes a goal to be met.

Faith is the substance of things hoped for. Let's say it another way. Faith is the substance of everything needed to accomplish the goal hoped for. That cooling unit has electricity connected to it **and is available at any time the thermostat makes a demand on it.**

That heating-cooling unit won't produce anything by itself. There must be a goal-setter, and you must dial the goal. Hope is a goal-setter for you. Always speak your hope.

Your goals for your heart are set by speaking those things in faith. Whether the unit feels like it or not, when that thermostat's impulse goes to that unit, it releases the energy that is available, and it immediately starts producing the thing you dialed into it.

Your Hope Makes Demands
by Being Spoken

That is the way the heart (spirit) of man works. You take the Word of God, and you speak it. You set the goal. The divine energy is in God's Word to cause the heart to produce. Even in the summertime, the energy that is bringing forth cool air in a building is the same energy that brings hot air in the wintertime.

The goal-setter (your hope) **is the thing that determines whether it is hot air or cool air.** If you're not satisfied with the harvest you're getting, **check up on the goal you're setting and the seed you're sowing.**

That unit won't argue with you. It's not designed to decide whether it's right or wrong. It's only designed to produce whatever you call for.

The heart of man works that way. Speaking the Word sets the goal. We have so separated natural things from spiritual things until most people believe there is no relationship between them. But Jesus brings them back together when He says, **"If you had faith like a mustard seed, you would say..."** (Luke 17:6 NASB).

Then in Genesis chapter eight, God says:

> **"While the earth remains, seedtime and harvest, cold and heat, winter and summer, and day and night shall not cease."**

Genesis 8:22

The Bible keeps referring to sowing. You sow the seed, you reap a harvest. **...** **Whatever a man sows, that he will also reap**. (Galatians 6:7). That's the way it works.

The soil in your garden doesn't decide whether or not what you plant is right or wrong. **The soil will produce whatever you plant in it.** Some believe that the human spirit, or the heart, of a born-again person would not produce anything bad. But ask yourself this question, "Why do some Christians sin?"

Jesus said it this way:

A good man out of the good treasure of his heart brings forth good things, and an evil man out of the evil treasure brings forth evil things.

Matthew 12:35

I am convinced from what Jesus taught that even a person who is born again can put evil things in his heart. God considers anything that is contrary to His Word to be evil. (Numbers 13:32). James said it this way:

If anyone among you thinks he is religious, and does not bridle his tongue but deceives his own heart, this one's religion *is* useless.

James 1:26

In other words, your tongue can deceive your heart.

The Soil Never Argues

I was a farmer for 30 years before I went into the ministry. Never in all the years that I farmed did I plant soybeans and hear the ground say to me, "We aren't going to raise soybeans, we're going to raise cucumbers and bananas," because the soil has no choice but to produce what is planted. Hope causes you to speak your faith.

But some have gotten the idea that it doesn't matter what they sow and it doesn't matter what they say. "Well, God knows what I meant," they say.

Would you say, "I planted radishes, but the soil knew what I meant; I meant to plant tomatoes"?

Certainly not. No one would be that foolish in the natural. You would know you were not going to raise tomatoes, because the soil doesn't produce what you *meant* but what you *planted.*

The soil of your heart does not decide whether what you plant (say) is right or wrong. Its job is to produce the information needed to cause what you are saying (planting) to come to pass, whether it is right, wrong, or indifferent.

Mark 11:23 is not a one-way street. But Jesus only told us how to operate faith on the positive side. He didn't want us to operate the principle on the negative side.

> **For assuredly, I say to you, whoever says to this mountain, "Be removed and be cast into the sea," and does not doubt in his heart, but believes that those things he says will be done, he will have whatever he says.**

Mark 11:23

Another Way to Say It

Believe that those things you sow will come to pass, because the saying is the sowing.

The goal is to be set on removing the mountain or the tremendous problems you face. Your hope then will cause you to speak your faith. On the other hand, it will work just as fast on the negative side. Some say, "This mountain is getting bigger every day. I'll never get over it."

They are right, because they are working the principle on the negative side. It will work just as quickly - and sometimes quicker - on the negative side.

Some prophesy that "Things are getting worse. We'll never make it. We'll never pay our debts. We'll never get this church going." They have no hope, so there is nothing to which faith can give substance.

They are speaking that into their soil (heart). It will cause their spirit to search the avenues of God's wisdom to find a way to bring it to pass.

Remember, the unit won't decide whether you need heat or cold, it only responds to the signal sent from the goal-setter. *Hope is the thermostat for your heart.* If you have no hope, no impulse is sent to the heart, and there will be no positive production.

Even though there is substance in the heart (faith), without **hope** there is no positive goal. **Hope causes you to speak**

the promise. Fear causes you to speak the worst of everything.

Remember, it is not going to work just because you say it, but saying it is involved in working God's principle, and it will eventually produce the results God promised.

Several years ago, when I saw this truth, I started saying, "I am redeemed from the curse. In the name of Jesus, I forbid sickness to operate in my body." At that time, I had ulcers. Every so often, I would be laid up for two or three days a week and couldn't do anything. I drank Maalox by the bottle.

Then I started speaking what God's Word said concerning my healing. Over a period of about three months, the Word of God was engrafted into my spirit and the ulcers left my body. They tried to come back a few times, but I would say, **"No, in the name of Jesus, I have received my healing."** I am healed. I am well. I am delivered from the curse of sickness. I continue to resist sickness like I resist the devil.

Conception Necessary
Before Manifestation

I learned how to operate in these principles through trial and error. I made some mistakes, but I continued to confess in faith that I am redeemed from the curse.

I declared, "I am redeemed from poison ivy." But when I came into contact with poison ivy, it would get on me. Just about every time I went deer hunting, I got poison ivy. Someone said, "It is not working, is it?"

I would reply, "Yes, it's working. Faith is coming. Faith is coming."

I was setting the goal. I kept saying it. What happened? I got poison ivy again!

What did I do? I put Calamine lotion on it, and it dried up and I continued declaring, "I am redeemed from poison ivy." This happened several times before the manifestation came. It took time to conceive the Word in my heart and cause faith to come.

Faith in the heart gives it the ability to conceive God's promise. Once it is conceived, you will eventually have a manifestation of that promise.

This continued for about a year and then I noticed that poison ivy didn't affect me anymore. The action that I took in agreement with what I believed was that I continued to say it, even though natural circumstances indicated that I was not redeemed from it. I just kept saying what God's Word said: "I was redeemed from the curse, according to Galatians 3:13 and Deuteronomy 28:61."

God's Word Is Over All Matter

Some people say, "That is mind over matter!" But it's not. **It's faith in God and His Word over all matter.**

When it was conceived in my spirit, it manifested itself in my physical body. At first, if the action I had taken was to pull poison ivy off the trees with my bare hands, I would have been in trouble, because I was just beginning to set the goal and sow the Word into my heart.

I didn't have full agreement between what I was saying and how my body reacted until I had the full manifestation. After about a year, poison ivy didn't affect my body. Now **my faith, belief and action toward poison ivy are the same.** My skin does not react to it. But it took about a year to conceive God's Word to the point that Galatians 3:13 was manifest in my body.

These things are not going to happen overnight. But they will happen, if we are diligent to agree with God and say what He said about us.

Confession Is a Process

Confession or speaking in agreement with God's Word is a process of renewing the mind. It causes faith to come. It is an expression of your hope. The heart conceives the promise you are speaking and brings the manifestation. This is the way it works in your physical body, in your finances, and in other situations of life.

But it takes time. It is a process. This is not a fad. This is a way of life. This is not something you try. If you are just going to try it, it won't work for you. If I had been trying it, then the first time I got poison ivy, I would have said, "It doesn't work." But it never occurred to me that it might not work, because Jesus had said that it would.

Practice Increases Production

Once you have found these Bible principles, study them and practice them. Don't back off from them when things appear to get worse. Just stay with it and keep saying it until it develops faith on the inside of you.

That doesn't mean that you wouldn't use medicine, if it's necessary. Yes, I used Calamine lotion. I took Maalox and everything else I could find to keep the symptoms down until I received the manifestation. Some well-meaning Christians have made the mistake of discontinuing their medicine before the manifestation of healing appeared in their body, thinking that this would force healing to occur.

Don't judge or condemn yourself or think you do not have enough faith because you take medicine. And don't allow others opinions to force you into trying to operate on <u>their</u> level of faith. Medicine won't heal you, but it will keep the symptoms under control until healing is manifest.

Let's say it this way: **Medicine won't heal you, and it won't keep you from being healed.** Remember: **Faith and hope are partners and you need them both.**

Start where you are. Use some common sense. Operate on your level of faith. Confess God's promises daily. Your faith will grow and your productivity will increase.

Charles Capps a farmer from England, Arkansas became an internationally known Bible teacher by sharing practical truths from the Word of God. His simplistic, down to earth style of applying spiritual principles to daily  life has appealed to people from every Christian denomination.

The requests for speaking engagements became so great after the printing of God's Creative Power® Will Work for You© that he retired from farming and became a full-time Bible teacher. His books are available in multiple languages throughout the world.

Besides publishing 24 books, including best-sellers The Tongue A Creative Force and God's Creative Power® series which has sold over 6 million copies, Capps Ministries has a national daily radio broadcast and weekly TV broadcast called "Concepts of Faith".

For a complete list of CDs, DVDs, and books
by Charles Capps, or to receive his
publication, Concepts of Faith, write:

Charles Capps Ministries

P.O. Box 69, England, Arkansas 72046

Toll Free Order Line (24 hours)

1-877-396-9400
www.charlescapps.com

BOOKS BY CHARLES CAPPS
AND ANNETTE CAPPS

Angels

God's Creative Power® for Finances

God's Creative Power® - Gift Edition
(Also available in Spanish)

BOOKS BY ANNETTE CAPPS

Quantum Faith®

*Reverse The Curse in
Your Body and Emotions*

Understanding Persecution

BOOKS BY CHARLES CAPPS

Triumph Over The Enemy

When Jesus Prays Through You

The Tongue – A Creative Force

Releasing the Ability of God Through Prayer

End Time Events

Your Spiritual Authority

Changing the Seen and Shaping The Unseen

Faith That Will Not Change

Faith and Confession

God's Creative Power® Will Work For You
(Also available in Spanish)

God's Creative Power® For Healing
(Also available in Spanish)

Success Motivation Through the Word

God's Image of You

Seedtime and Harvest
(Also available in Spanish)

The Thermostat of Hope
(Also available in Spanish)

The Tongue – A Creative Force – Gift Edition

How You Can Avoid Tragedy

Kicking Over Sacred Cows

The Substance of Things

The Light of Life in the Spirit of Man

Faith That Will Work For You

Powerful Teaching From Charles Capps

If you have enjoyed reading this book, you can find more dynamic teaching from Charles Capps in these revolutionary books.

Can Your Faith Fail?

Faith That Will Not Change

Have you ever stepped out in faith only to later feel that you have failed? If you are like most Christians, at some point in your life, you have questioned the word God gave you. The truth, however, is that faith is a law and God's laws always work. This is a practical guide to encourage you in your walk with God. It will teach you how to put your faith into action to produce results in your life.

ISBN-13: 978-0-9819574-6-3

You Can Change
The Direction of Your Life

How You Can Avoid Tragedy
And Live A Better Life

How often have you heard the question: "They were such good Christians! Why did this happen to them?" Many believers' lives have been overwhelmed needlessly by defeat and tragedy.

Satan's greatest weapon has been deception - getting you to believe something contrary to God's Word. Wrong speaking, wrong praying, and wrong believing will destroy your faith. Praying "If it be Thy Will," has opened doors for the devil's opportunity when God's Will is already revealed in His Word.

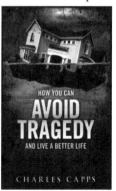

ISBN-13: 978-0-9819574-5-6

Understanding Paul's "Thorn In The Flesh" And How You Can Overcome The Messenger Of Satan Assigned To You

Triumph Over The Enemy

In Second Corinthians 12:7, Paul writes about "a thorn in the flesh, the messenger of Satan" who had been sent to harass him. This "messenger" was sent to create problems and stir up the people against Paul everywhere he preached. But Paul knew the key to overcoming this obstacle – he learned to exercise his God-given authority here on the earth!

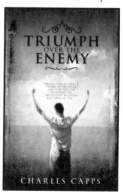

This book will show you how to walk in God's grace and triumph over this enemy sent to harass and keep you from God's greater blessings in your life.

ISBN-13: 978-0-9819574-2-5